STREET SURVIVAL GUIDE: SELF DEFENSE AWARENESS, AVOIDANCE AND FIGHTING TECHNIQUES

RORY CHRISTENSEN

Copyright © 2013 by Rory Christensen
All rights reserved.
This book or any portion thereof
may not be reproduced or used in any manner whatsoever
without the express written permission of the publisher
except for the use of brief quotations in a book review.

ONE

About Self Defense

Probably the number one reason most people take up the martial arts is to learn how to defend themselves if ever the need arises. Many consider self-defense to be a vital and desirable skill to have in a society where violence and attacks on innocent people are the norm.

It seems every time we pick up a newspaper or watch television, we are bombarded by images of violence and stories of people getting attacked on the street or in their own homes, often for no other reason than they happened to be in the wrong place at the wrong time.

I am not of course suggesting that you will get attacked every time you step out your front door (or even when you close it behind you). What I am suggesting is that sometimes these incidents happen, often when we least expect them.

It is surely better to be prepared enough for such incidents that you can respond in a way that will save you from harm as opposed to not responding at all and perhaps, in a worst-case scenario, losing your life.

This book is therefore aimed at those who…

- Have no experience of self-defense training but want to learn.

- Have experience in self-defense but want to deepen their understanding and fill the gaps in their knowledge.

How Can You Learn self-defense From A Book?

This book assumes that you are already a practicing martial artist, or if not, that you intend to be one. It is preferable to learn the physical aspects of self-defense—the hard skills—in a dojo with a willing partner or partners. Failing that, any space will do, though obviously some environments will limit or hinder your practice. Try to find the most suitable practice space possible. Like all physical skills, the techniques described here have to be practiced over and over in order for you to use them effectively.

There are, however, plenty of concepts and mental aspects of self-defense that can be worked on outside the training place, and these are perhaps more important than learning the combat side of things.

So even if you read this book and don't implement the physical aspects described, you will still learn a lot on how to become more confident within yourself and implement positive changes that will dramatically reduce any fears of violence that you may have.

Self-defense is as much about changing your perspective on violence as it is about actually dealing with it when it happens. This book can help you do both. With that in mind, let's get started.

What Is self-defense?

Different people interpret the concept of self-defense in different ways, with most considering self-defense to be the act of defending oneself against a violent attack from another person or persons. While this is true to an extent, there is more to it than that.

Self-defense, as a concept, is about more than physical violence. It is also about taking measures to prevent such violence from happening in the first place. Prevention is 90% of what self-defense is all about, and it is something that will be covered at length later in this book.

Regardless of how you or I or anyone else defines self-defense, the only definition that really matters is the one set out by the law. Self-defense is a legally defined term, which means no one—martial arts instructors, magazine writers, book writers, or any other "expert" on the subject—gets to redefine it. It is what it is, and that's that.

So let's now look at how the law defines self-defense.

self-defense And The Law

According to the 'Lectric Law Library the law defines self-defense thus:

"Use of force is justified when a person reasonably believes that it is necessary for the defense of oneself or another against the immediate use of

unlawful force. However, a person must use no more force than appears reasonably necessary in the circumstances.

Force likely to cause death or great bodily harm is justified in self-defense only if a person reasonably believes that such force is necessary to prevent death or great bodily harm.

The right to protect one's person and property from injury."

From this definition, to plead self-defense, one must only be reacting to the actions of another. In other words, you can't be the aggressor in the situation.

What's also implicit here is that by pleading self-defense, you are also admitting to unlawful actions (i.e., bodily harm on another), and by doing so, it is now up to you to show that those actions were justified. If you cannot do so to a reasonable extent, you will be prosecuted for your actions.

But how do you know if your actions are justified or not? This is where it gets tricky. If you're attacked, you are legally required to do only enough to subdue the attack—to make it stop. Further to this, anything you do before the attack will have a bearing on the legal outcome. This means if you provoked someone into attacking you, then you will be viewed as the aggressor, and your plea for self-defense will be seriously undermined.

Doing anything to aggravate a situation that has turned violent, or going beyond the use of reasonable force, crosses the line into fighting as far as the law is concerned. Once again, you will be held liable for your actions.

. . .

So what is the difference between fighting and self-defense?

The Difference Between Fighting And self-defense

Here is a dictionary definition of fighting:

"To attempt to harm or gain power over an adversary by blows or with weapons.

To contend with physically or in battle. To wage or carry on (a battle).
These definitions clearly show that fighting involves the willing participation of both parties."

In terms of a confrontation, true self-defense would involve running away from the encounter instead of willingly entering it.

This often poses a problem for people who are trained in martial arts. Many martial artists will refuse to run or avoid a confrontation because pride and a need to prove themselves get in the way. They therefore end up fighting instead of defending themselves.

When the law gets involved, and it realizes you did nothing to back away from the confrontation, it will assume you had motivation to stay and therefore, motivation to escalate the situation.

As far as the law is concerned then, these are not the actions of a reasonable person interested in defending themselves. These are, in fact, the actions of someone who has reason and motivation to stay and engage in conflict.

. . .

It can be seen that self-defense as far as the law is concerned is not cut and dried. It is a legal minefield that will drag you down if you're not careful. If you find the whole thing confusing, that's because it is (as most things to do with the law are).

You may be wondering now what the right approach to self-defense would be. Let's try to work that out.

What Is The Right Approach To self-defense?
Even though there are many factors to consider from a legal standpoint, I believe that with self-defense, there are two things you can do to at least try to keep yourself right if the law gets involved (which it inevitably will).

1. Don't Be An Aggressor. Do nothing to provoke an attack or aggravate that attack when it happens. This includes verbal provocation.

2. Don't Over React. Do only what is necessary to subdue the attack. Anything after this is seen as unnecessary force, and you will be once again be viewed as an aggressor and judged guilty of fighting.

Follow these two simple rules and stay on the right side of the law.

Now, having said all that, there is a flip-side. Contemplating the legal repercussions of defending yourself can be very unwise because it can cause indecision, which will inevitably lead to defeat.

In the end, you do what you have to do to stop the attack, even if that means stepping past boundaries set in place by the law. It's your life at risk, and that is more important than any law. As the saying goes, it's better to be judged by twelve than carried by six.

. . .

Street Survival Guide: Self Defense Awareness, Avoidance And Fighting...

We will continue to look at the legal aspects of self-defense throughout the rest of this book and how they relate to the rest of the information contained within these pages. You will find them easier to understand when they are put in context.

For now, let us move on to probably the most important aspect of self-defense that you should learn, and that is prevention.

TWO

Prevention Tactics

As we have already said, prevention is probably the most essential thing to know and learn for self-defense. If you can prevent an attack from happening in the first place, you won't have to worry about getting hurt or caught up in the legal system.

If you learn nothing else from this book except what is explained in this section, then your time will not have been wasted. The knowledge and advice given in this part of the book will save you a lot of trouble in the long run if you follow it and integrate it into your daily life.

Prevention of violence involves having the right mentality and using your common sense, two elementary concepts that a staggering number of people do not abide by. If everyone took advantage of the power they possess for prevention, there would be a lot less violent attacks taking place in society.

I believe we construct our own reality, which is why we will take a brief look at the law of attraction (bear with me, this has nothing to do with *The Secret* or any similar garbage).

The Law Of Attraction

The law of attraction states that we attract into our life what we most emotively think about. So in this context, if you think about violence all the time, you will inevitably attract violence into your life.

If you constantly live in fear of being attacked, if you constantly dwell on the fact that you might be attacked the next time you step outside your house, the likelihood is that this will happen at some point.

This is the law of the universe.

If you want to avoid violence, or at least drastically reduce your chances of encountering it, then stop thinking about it.

It is easy, in this media-driven age, to get paranoid and worried about all the violence in the world. Wrong thinking can make you go out and buy guns, have weapons in every room in your house, carry knives on your person.

And for what? To protect you against something that is statistically very unlikely to happen?

Such behavior will make these things happen if you are not careful.

To paraphrase Bruce Lee, it is the art of fighting without fighting.

We live in a violent world. That doesn't mean you have to dwell on the fact and worry yourself sick over it. Be prepared to counter violence if it comes your way, but don't worry about it outside of training.

Your mentality in your everyday life is important, and that's what we shall discuss now.

The Victim Mentality And How To Avoid It

Victims are what predators look for when they search for prey.

What is a victim? A victim is someone who looks like easy prey, someone who does not pose a threat and can be easily dominated and controlled.

Victims do not fight back, and predators know this. Essentially, your average street thug wants to feel good about themselves by aggressively dominating someone weaker than them.

A street thug does not want someone who will stand up to them or try to fend them off, because then the thug loses control of the situation. Which is what it is all about—power and control.

Bullies crave that sense of power more than anything. The more dominant they are over their victims, the greater sense of power they will feel.

It makes sense then that the less like a victim you come across, the more likely it is that bullies and thugs will leave you alone.

If you do not change your way of thinking and rid yourself of your victim mentality, you will be plagued your whole life by bullies who think they have a right to walk over you whenever they please, and this applies to other areas of your life as well, like at work and home. There are plenty of ways to victimize someone without inflicting violence on them.

Either way, don't give bullies a chance. Learn to give of the signal that you are not a pushover and that you won't be easily messed with.

But how do you stop being a victim? Taking up martial arts is a good way to quash the victim mentality because martial arts training is very empowering in that way. It can make you mentally and physically tough, and this toughness will shine through when you walk down the street.

Besides that, there is also a process of preliminary self-defense that you can learn, and that will help you no end in avoiding any kind of violence for the rest of your life.

I have come up with what I like to call the three A's to explain the process.

In short, the three A's are: **attitude, awareness, action.**

Three simple steps that will give you the tools you need to help you avoid any future confrontations out on the street.

Let's look at the three A's and see how you can apply them to your life.

Attitude

• • •

The correct attitude is the single biggest attribute you must possess to keep yourself out of needless trouble.

You can't think like a victim. If you do, it will show in your body language, and body language is all-important in the street environment.

If you are to avoid trouble, you cannot walk down the street with your head down and your shoulders slumped with hands dug deep into your pockets. You cannot look timid.

Someone looking for a fight will most often go for the person who looks the least threatening, the person who will not fight back. Thugs prey on the weak and the timid.

If you are the type of person whose body language screams victim, then you will get picked on a lot. Thugs are very good at sizing up potential prey to have some fun with. Do you really want to be some thug's plaything that gets discarded afterward and left in a bloody mess? Of course you don't. So how can you stop this from happening?

The surest way is to change the message you give out when you walk down the street.

Change your way of thinking and acting.

For a start, stop feeling like a victim and refuse to be intimidated by anyone, no matter what size they are or how many of them there are.

• • •

But how do you do you make a stand against such people?

Well, first, you change the way you think about yourself. Start developing your confidence. If you do martial arts, you should be taking a lot of confidence from your training. You know a bit about how to handle yourself, so this should be enough to boost your confidence and change your victim mentality.

The most significant change the martial arts had on me was the way it changed how I thought about myself and the way I presented myself to the world. I gained enough inner-strength from the training to allow me to walk down the street and put out the vibe that I wouldn't be messed with.

You should do the same.

Decide right now that you will never be messed with by anyone again because no one will dare because of your skills, and if they do, then God help them. This is the way you have to think.

This doesn't mean you have to walk down the street like the Terminator, eye-balling everyone around and daring them to have a go if they are hard enough.

What I am talking about is more subtle than that. I'm asking you to cultivate a state of mind that will eventually build into quiet confidence as opposed to any kind of arrogance or even, God forbid, aggressiveness.

Give off just enough of a vibe so that predators will quickly dismiss you as being unsuitable prey.

. . .

They will pass you by because you won't fit the victim profile.

This change in attitude will do wonders for you in the long run. You'll feel safer within yourself because you know that you are no longer a victim, and you are not anyone's idea of easy prey.

Carry yourself with your head held high and radiate the quiet confidence we just talked about, and you won't go far wrong.

Awareness

You can be as confident and as self-assured as you can be, but it's no good if you are going to keep walking into trouble all the time. A good sense of awareness is therefore vital to you avoiding any potentially violent altercations.

I would describe awareness as having the ability to spot any potentially dangerous situations. This means you have to be streetwise as much as possible.

Walking alone in areas that have a reputation for violence is a good example of not being fully aware. If you were aware of the dangers involved in walking down dodgy streets, you probably wouldn't do so, and even if you did, you would at least be privy to the possibility that you might be in danger.

Make it your business to have some working knowledge of the places you frequent. Leave yourself open to the possibility that you could run into trouble. That way, if the worst happens, then at least it won't come as a complete shock.

Believe me, any violent altercation is shocking enough without coming totally from left-field. If a part of you is ready to deal with something like that, you stand a much better chance of surviving it—a lot more than you would if you were not expecting it.

A note of caution here. There is a fine line between awareness and full-blown paranoia. It is crucial that you realize this. Your level of awareness has to be low enough that it is almost unconscious and high enough that you are aware of your surroundings.

It's all about balance. If you dwell on the fact that you might run into trouble, there is a better-than-average chance that you will eventually do just that. Eventually, you will see trouble around every corner. Such an outlook is not good for your mental well-being as you will be in a constant state of tension, walking around like a coiled spring all the time.

Allow your awareness to become subconscious so it is always there, turned on, but not so conscious that you can't think of anything else. After a while, you will get good at sizing up people and situations. You will be able to quickly and accurately assess the threat level in any situation.

Your intuition will guide you in this respect if you let it. Your intuition will let you know what awareness level you have to be at. It rises and falls accordingly.

It will remain low when you are walking down the street, rise as a drunk guy with an angry look on his face comes towards you, lowers when he passes by, rises again when you realize someone is walking behind you, lowers again when you turn round and realize it is just an old lady. And so forth.

Don't forget common sense here. Don't be stupid enough to venture into known trouble spots. Don't hang around clubs or bars after closing unless you like drunken brawling. Avoid needlessly antagonizing people. Common sense. Get some, it's great, it's free, and it saves you lots of trouble.

So be aware, but don't be a paranoid wreck.

Action

Your awareness level is through the roof. There will definitely be trouble, and there's no getting away from it. What are you going to do?

Having awareness is nothing without the ability to act on it quickly and decisively. If you will not make some kind of proactive response to the situation you find yourself in, you may as well have not even noticed the situation. All your carefully cultivated awareness will have been for nothing.

The action you take will depend on the situation. If you suddenly happen upon a gang of thugs hanging around a street corner, your action can be as simple as crossing the road to avoid them or just strolling past them confidently, giving off the vibe that you are not what they are looking for.

On the other hand, you may find yourself being provoked and threatened to where you have no choice but to stand and face your aggressor. Despite your best efforts, you are being forced into a full-blown confrontation. What type of action do you now take?

There are many forms of action you can take at this stage of the game, depending on the exact circumstances you find yourself in. Let's now look at the confrontation stage and where we go from there.

THREE

Self Defense Psychology

If you aim to avoid violence, it helps to know a little about the psychology behind it. If you know why, where, and how an attack is likely to happen, it is easier to avoid such situations in the first place or, at the very least, prepare for them.

Before you can do that, though, you have to know what to look for and the warning signs that signal a potential threat.

The Four "D"s

The four "D"s are techniques often used by attackers to prepare their victims for assault. Even though these techniques are very common precepts to violent assault, most people aren't aware of them.

If you are serious about making yourself a hard target for potential attackers, familiarize yourself with these techniques.

Muggers and the like often use dialogue to disarm and distract potential victims. They will approach their chosen victim and engage them in some innocuous conversation, such as asking for a light, seeking directions, or just asking if you have the time.

While they have your attention, you do not see the weapon they produce or their mate coming around behind you to attack.

Just by understanding the purpose of this ritual, you can stay switched on and alert, giving you a better chance at pre-empting the ritual before it escalates into assault.

Deception

Deception is an attacker's greatest weapon, and they will often use it to make themselves appear harmless. They will come across as being relatively unassuming in appearance, and will often be polite in the way they speak to you. All of this is designed to sucker you in so you will let down your guard and give them a window of opportunity in which to attack.

Distraction is usually accomplished through dialogue. An attacker may ask you a question to engage your brain for a second, at which point they will attack.

Such distraction will also switch off any instinctive physical response that you may have, creating a "blind second,"—a second of time when you have no awareness.

You won't be thinking about a physical response while you are thinking about what directions to give or what the time is.

It's a simple ploy, but highly effective.

Even if you put up a fence straight away, a cunning attacker will feign submissiveness or try to shake your hand, anything to get you to drop your guard so they can attack.

I used to see this all the time when I was bouncing. Guy's would act all submissive and ask to shake your hand, telling you there were no hard feelings, but all they wanted to do was shove a glass in your face when you stretched your hand out.

Never give in to this sort of pleading.

Destruction

This is the final "D" and the result of the initial priming with the other three "D"s. If you let the ritual get this far, it is safe to assume that you won't expect the first blow, and that will be enough to put you down where your attacker wants you.

No matter how experienced a fighter you are, if you allow yourself to be suckered in by deception and distraction, destruction will be the inevitable result.

Once again, if you stay switched on to this behavior, there will be less chance of you being deceived in this way.

It's also worth mentioning here that these tricks can be used against an attacker as well. What works against you can also be used by you. Employing deception by using dialogue or some other distraction in the run-up to your escape from a situation or just before you strike an attacker can be very useful and should be mandatory techniques in your arsenal.

The Eye Contact Challenger

Eyeballing, as it's known in some places around the world, is the act of staring at someone in a hostile and confrontational manner. To eyeball someone is to try to assert your dominance over the other person and let them know that you are up for a scrap.

It's the most common way of displaying overt aggression from a distance which is why the "eye contact challenger" (as Geoff Thompson calls them in his book, *Dead or Alive*) is the most common type of adversary you will face in bars and clubs and sometimes on the street.

It is therefore worth familiarizing yourself with this type of challenger and the rituals they often exhibit just before an attack.

It is common when you're out to make eye contact with people, accidentally or otherwise, and if you are not careful, a casual glance initially can often lead to a fight.

As a bouncer, I saw this kind of thing regularly. Two people would often stare each other out from a distance before moving in towards each other for an argument that would quickly escalate into physical violence.

This kind of thing can be easily avoided on your part if you know what to look for. The kinds of people who look to make eye contact so they can start a fight with someone are easily spotted in a crowded bar or club. They often have an arrogant gait and come across as being quite aggressive as they stand at the bar staring around them. They will also often walk the "hard man walk," with arms held out like they are carrying a fridge under each arm.

Every bar and club in the world has at least one idiot that will fit this description. If you remain in code yellow (as you should be doing), these people are easy to spot, and you can avoid them.

If you make eye contact with such a person, don't allow your ego to draw you into a staring match, because that's what they want. Look away and put as much distance between yourself and them as possible.

Eye contact challengers want you to hold their stare so they can initiate aggressive dialogue. They will often ask you what you are looking at or what your problem is. The pre-fight dialogue has then started.

In my experience, if you retaliate with dialogue of your own, you will worsen the situation. It is usually best to say nothing and walk away. Your challenger will then see this as a submission on your part, and they will have won, at least in their small minds.

Further trouble can usually be avoided in this way. Trouble usually only starts when you can't resist the urge to square off to these people and bite back.

Again, this is your ego leading you by the hand here. It's up to you to control it if you don't want to be fighting.

If you retaliate to his verbal challenge, expect to be approached physically.

Once you've been approached, your challenger will then usually repeat their question. *"I said, what the fuck are you looking at?"*

. . .

From here, an actual challenge is then thrown down. *"You want to go then, do you?"*

At this point, your challenger will begin to talk in single syllables as they move closer to you, preparing to attack. Words such as *"yeah"*, *"so"* and *"and"* or often used, which is a sure sign that the interview is coming to an end, and violence is looming.

Also, look out for signs of adrenaline on your challenger's part, such as arm splaying, eye bulge, neck pecking, finger beckoning, and distance close-down as they move steadily towards you.

Distance close-down, in my experience, is usually a guarantee that things will kick off almost immediately. This is where your fence comes in to protect your personal space.

Depending on your response to any of these things, parts of this ritual may be overlooked as your challenger hastens their attack.

Like I've already said, don't let things get that far. Carry yourself with a confident gait (even if you don't feel confident), and most would-be attackers will leave you alone.

Confident people are generally not chosen for attack unless things are personal. If you catch someone's eye, look away and don't get drawn into a staring match that might lead to physical violence.

Don't Take It Personally

I believe that most unprovoked violence is down to displaced aggression on the part of the attacker. If these people were happy in themselves, they wouldn't be so quick to attack other people.

When they attack other people, they are really attacking themselves and whatever is wrong in their life.

This displaced aggression is often exacerbated by alcohol and drugs, both of which make it easy for attackers to tap into their latent violent streak.

So if you find yourself on the receiving end of such violent aggression, it would be wrong to look for a reason for it or take it personally.

People who are attacked often agonize over why someone would do that to them, trying to find some sort of logic behind it when there is none.

The truth is, they were just another target for someone to take their frustrations out on.

So don't take it personally. It isn't you. It's them.

Stay Switched On And Make Yourself A Hard Target

Most of the advice I've given you here is just common sense. If you stay switched on enough as you go about your business, you should have no problems spotting the various attack rituals that attackers often use to get around people.

Practice target hardening. If you are approached by a stranger, make sure you "stance up" before giving the time or directions. That way, you won't be caught off guard if you are attacked.

Similarly, stay away from places that have a reputation for trouble. Avoid walking alone down secluded areas at night. Just use your common sense and carry yourself in a confident manner at all times, so you will be less likely to be chosen as a victim by potential attackers.

It always comes down to awareness.

Attacks usually only happen to people who are switched off and haven't made themselves a hard target.

Don't be one of those people.

FOUR

Confrontation

Sometimes, despite all your best efforts to avoid any kind of violent confrontation, you will find yourself face to face with an aggressor intent on making trouble for you. This does not mean you just have to get tore into them straight away, for as we have already discussed, this could be a mistake. Doing so means you will end up fighting, and this is the last thing you want to have to do.

Fortunately, there are other options that you can explore before it gets to that stage, which we will now look at.

Swallow Your Pride And Run!

Yes, run.

Why would you want to hang around long enough for something to happen?

. . .

If you see a chance at escape, then take it. Don't think about it—just do it!

Why?

Because then you won't have to fight and risk getting injured or worse.

Many people, especially those with martial arts training, will feel the need to stand their ground and take on whatever comes their way. Pride gets in the way.

What kind of man will I be if I run away?

This a common question people often ask themselves when someone wants to fight them or verbally humiliate them. That is your ego talking, not your survival instinct. You'll be more of a man if you get yourself out of harm's way instead of foolishly putting yourself directly in it.

Maybe you think you have something to prove.

If you're a martial artist and you have all those years of training behind you, then you will probably think to yourself, what's the point of all that training if I can't put it to the test? I can take this guy. Why should I let him get away with provoking me?

Again, that's your ego talking.

That you feel you have to prove yourself by staying to fight shows that you have insecurity issues. If you have such issues, I suggest you examine them and find a way to work them out. Otherwise, they will get you in needless trouble someday.

. . .

How silly would you feel if one day you got carted off in an ambulance because you were too full of pride or you let your ego get the better of you?

Guaranteed, you'll be riding along in the back of that ambulance, perhaps with a close friend or family member lying hurt beside you, cursing yourself for not running away when you had the chance.

Even if you come out unscathed, you will still, as we have already discussed, have to deal with the law.

Why would you want that?

So you dropped the guy in one shot. Big deal. How full of pride will you be when he tries to sue you for breaking his jaw?

Think all the time. Keep your wits about you and decide on a course of action that will cause you the least amount of hassle. You can run in one direction and have no trouble, or you can face the other direction and open a can of worms that might come back to haunt you. It's up to you.

Fear and How To Manage It

Fear is a constant companion for most people, especially in today's urban environment, where violence and confrontation are the norms.

Out of all the emotions one can have, most people know fear the best because it has such a powerful influence on us. To have a life without fear in it is almost impossible for most people to imagine and it is not one you should try to imagine for fear is a constant of the human condition; it's as much a part of us as any other emotion and to try to rid yourself permanently of it is a fruitless endeavor.

That's the thing about fear—it never goes away!

But rather than let this get you down, start to see fear as a necessary emotion and one which you should learn to use to your advantage rather than let it negatively impact you.

Fear can be a powerful tool that will aid us in our response to confrontation, and we should attempt to get to know it so we can better channel its energy into positive action.

That's what this part of the book will aim to show you—how to turn an emotion that most people see as negative into something positive and useful.

First, let us first get clear on what exactly fear is and the impact it can have on us.

What Is Fear?

The English dictionary tells us that fear is:

"An unpleasant, often strong emotion caused by anticipation or awareness of danger."

When the brain senses danger it triggers adrenalin which triggers the fight-or-flight response—a massive dump of adrenaline that can be felt in the pit of the stomach and which urges us to react either way to the perceived danger—you either stay and confront it (fight) or you run away from it (flight).

The problem with this reaction is that it often causes terror immobilization or the "freeze syndrome" in people. You end up rooted to the spot, unable to move or make any clear decisions as to what to do next. This is why so many people view fear as a negative response because of the debilitating effect it has on them.

The effect is only debilitating if you let it be, though. By releasing so much adrenaline from the adrenal gland into the system, your body is trying to help you.

For a short time, your whole body will become turbocharged and ready for action. You will feel stronger, faster, and your body will be partially anesthetized to pain, making you better able to handle a violent confrontation.

So if the fight-or-flight reaction is helpful to us in certain situations, why do so many of us view it as being bad?

The reason for that is that people have not trained themselves to react positively to the response and end up falling into a state of panic, caused when the reasoning process mistakes adrenalin for fear.

This leaves a person drained of all that good energy and often frozen in fear in the face of the ensuing danger.

Adrenalin can also be released into the body in different ways, the two most important of which for our purposes are slow-release and immediate-release.

· · ·

A slow release of adrenalin occurs when you anticipate confrontation and the adrenaline is released slowly, sometimes over months, so you end up feeling constant anxiety and what you perceive to be as fear over the expected event which can be anything from a martial arts grading or competition, to a public speaking event, to an important business meeting.

An immediate or fast release of adrenalin occurs when anticipation is not present, or a situation escalates unexpectedly fast, causing an adrenal dump, as psychologists like to call it. The feeling is often so intense that a person will freeze in the face of confrontation because they mistake the feeling for sheer terror.

Within that, there are also secondary occurrences of adrenalin that happen in a situation when things are not going to plan, or you start to anticipate the consequences of a situation. Again, your body is just trying to help you along by doing this, not immobilize you with fear.

The sooner you start to recognize and acknowledge the adrenal response for what it is—a means to help you—the sooner you can begin to deal with your fear.

We have been conditioned, both by ourselves and by other people over the years to accept fear as something that is there to hold us back and stop us from doing the things we want to do, when in fact fear exists to help us do the things we want to do because it readies our bodies and minds for action.

This is especially true with street self-defense when we think we are feeling terror, but it's just the process of our bodies becoming primed to deal with the situation.

Bodyguards don't call the adrenal dump the "wow factor" for nothing. They know it's just the juice they need to carry them through a dangerous situation.

. . .

You should look at fear in the same way. Condition yourself to recognize the signs, to expect them, and then to use them in how they are supposed to be used.

Don't think of fear as fear, think of it as super-fuel that turbocharges you into action. It's there for a reason, and there isn't another substance on the planet that will so effectively help you in this way.

Why should you be afraid when you have such powerful resources at your disposal?

So bearing all that in mind, let's now look at a technique that will allow you to control a potentially violent situation before it gets out of hand.

The Fence

Okay, you've exhausted all avenues of escape. There's nowhere to run. What now?

Even at this stage of the game, you don't have to get violent just yet. You still have options, and the fence is one of them.

The fence is a self-defense technique made famous by self-defense expert Geoff Thompson, and it is a means for you to subtly control an opponent without them hardly even knowing they are being controlled.

In one sense, the fence is a straightforward technique to use. All you do is take a small 45-degree stance that is as inconspicuous as possible. Your arms are out in front of you, palms open as you control that all-important gap between you and your opponent.

. . .

Try not to make physical contact at this stage because this can antagonize an opponent and make them aggressive.

The whole time you do this, try to talk your opponent down while being careful not to antagonize them. This means not getting into staring matches or using provocative language.

You are trying to calm them down while also placing yourself in an ideal position to react if they try to attack you. By controlling them in this way, you are also controlling the distance between you and them, making it hard for them to lunge at you or kick you suddenly. That's the simple explanation of the fence.

The reality of using it is slightly different and takes a lot of practice to get right.

When you apply the fence in a situation, do it as naturally as possible so that your opponent is not aware, on a conscious level, that you are trying to control them. They will know in the back of their minds that this is what you are doing, but they won't be able to do anything about it, providing you are doing the technique correctly.

You must always move your hands around his arms and in front of his body, continually controlling the distance between you and preventing him from making any surprise attacks.

If the moment comes when he attacks, say with a punch, you are in the right position to block his attack and counter with one of your own. A punch to the jaw is a good counter move because it will daze if not drop him right there, giving you time to run in the confusion.

. . .

The fence is a skill that must be practiced often in order to master it. It is not something that can be mastered overnight.

The real skill lies in making your controlling movements seem natural and unforced. If an opponent becomes aware that you are trying to control them, they will react against that by becoming more violent.

The fence is essential because it can put you in a position where you are in full control of the situation and are thus not at the mercy of your opponent's violent temper.

This alone will give you a lot of confidence in dealing with potential attackers because you know you have the means to control and contain them and also react quickly if need be.

Having this knowledge will do wonders for your overall confidence and reinforce your attitude, making sure you never sink into the victim mentality we talked about earlier.

FIVE

Basic Strategies and Techniques

It is well beyond the scope of this book to include every self-defense tactic and strategy there is, simply because there are so many of them, especially techniques.

For every attack you can think of, there are dozens of different responses to it. This isn't always a good thing, for you can end up with "technique log jam," and it will hinder your response time to an attack.

That's why in this section, I'm just going to concentrate on the more basic strategies and techniques that you can use in most if not all the situations you may one day find yourself in.

The only way to go further into this and deepen your knowledge is by training in some kind of martial art if you are not already doing so. Training in the martial arts will teach you about timing, distance, basic strikes and takedowns, throws, locks, everything you will need to defend yourself on the street.

. . .

Training for self-defense

For quite a long time in my training career, I labored under the illusion that the methods of training I was using were preparing me to deal with actual violent encounters and combat outside the dojo.

For many years I trained in traditional arts, diligently practicing techniques that I was told would help me if someone tried to attack me, and I pretty much believed this to be true.

I thought if I practiced the techniques enough and with enough intent behind them each time I did them, then eventually, I would be good enough to handle anyone who ever tried to attack me.

God help anyone who ever tried to lay a finger on me because I would just react with one of the great techniques I had been shown and that would be it, the show would be over, and I'd stroll on home feeling lethal and pleased with myself. That's how I thought, anyway.

Then I got a job as a bouncer and realized that I would never be able to effectively use the vast majority of the techniques I had been shown.

Very quickly, I realized that I had been training away in a blissful cloud of ignorance, utterly blinkered to the goings-on in the concrete dojo.

There was nothing fancy about the real world of violence. It was brutal, and it was very goddamn scary.

In that job, being proficient in martial arts—mainly traditional martial arts—was both a blessing and a hindrance. I wasn't the biggest bouncer in the world. Indeed, I was a lightweight compared to most of the guys I ended up working with, so I wasn't very physically intimidating, and I knew this.

So I took confidence from the fact that I was better trained than most of the people I would be coming into contact with. This allowed me to think I could do the job. It gave me just enough credibility to get by. The rest I would get by proving myself capable of the job by doing it right. So my martial arts training was a blessing in that respect.

I soon realized, though, that it was also a hindrance, and this happened when it became clear that I would never be able to use most of what I knew.

I got caught up in a nasty situation one night that involved eight big guys against three of us bouncers. I used a few techniques that were nowhere near as effective as I thought they would be, and the crushing fear of the situation made me back away when I shouldn't have.

On the whole, the experience was a complete eye-opener for me. I had never felt such adrenaline-induced fear in my life, a fear that rendered my oft-practiced techniques almost useless.

I had never trained for such a situation. In the dojo, the pressure I had previously felt was minuscule by comparison to the overwhelming stress I felt that night.

In the dojo, I felt calm and in control, powerful even.

That night, with the fists flying and the blood splattering, I felt like I was being controlled only by fear and that I was weak instead of powerful.

Years of training had practically come to nothing.

I stuck with the job for a while, though, because I thought the experience would be good for me, both personally and as a martial artist, which it was on both fronts.

The fear never really went away. Although I got better at handling situations, I never ceased to be afraid.

It wasn't until later, when I read Geoff Thompson's book *Fear*, that I realized this feeling of fear was natural and that everyone feels it.

You just have to learn how to control it.

I got in a few more scrapes while bouncing, and after each one, I got more used to the experience (exposure training) though never completely. From a performance point of view, I still needed a lot of work.
    Eventually, I quit bouncing because of the unsociable hours and because at times it felt like a prison sentence. A lot of bouncers get almost addicted to the job, and when they quit, they wonder why they ever did it for so long. I was in that group. I don't miss it.

The whole bouncing experience, though, taught me the genuine need for different training methods for street self-defense and actual combat.

The traditional methods of training had proved woefully inadequate. That's not to say that the training was a waste of time—it wasn't. The techniques just had to be modified to meet the demands of a high-pressure live situation.

So now, I strive to make my training as alive as possible. More and more, I have tried to move away from the static nature of traditional training methods (though not altogether, as I'll soon explain) and to make the training much more dynamic and realistic.

My new goal was to perform better, mentally and physically, in a combat situation and not to kid myself that just because I had trained extensively in martial arts that I would somehow naturally be able to handle a real attack.

I believe this is a fatal assumption that many martial artists make, and it takes a bit of humility and swallowing of pride to admit this to yourself. It did with me. I had to admit that I didn't know half as much as I thought I knew when it came to effective street self-defense.

Once you make this mental jump, however, you will come on leaps and bounds in terms of your training.

To paraphrase Bruce Lee, you will be emptying your cup of knowledge (what you think you know) to make way for new knowledge (what you should know).

Now you can really start to learn.

Sparring For Combat

In the vast majority of dojos across the globe, martial artists tend to spar the same way, which is to say that most of us spar for competition purposes.

There are always rules to abide by, and there are many techniques that can't be used for either safety reasons or reasons of style.

For example, when sparring for kickboxing, there is no grappling, only kicking and punching, and even these techniques are done in a very stylized way.

Even in MMA, which many would argue (wrongly in my view) is a close representation of street fighting, there are rules to follow, and there are safety measures in place to prevent injury to vital areas.
And once again, the fighting itself is very stylized and nothing like the chaotic nature of most street fights.

It is therefore wrong to assume that because you are good at sparring that you will also be good in a street fight. We can back this supposition up with a few more facts about street fighting. Consider that:

• Most street fights take place at close range, unlike most dojo sparring where the range is long.

• Real fights often involve multiple opponents and weapons, neither of which are factored into dojo sparring.

• Real fights are usually extremely fast, frantic, and sloppy, nothing as controlled as dojo sparring.

• Real fights are never the skilled exchange between martial artists that we see in the dojo.

. . .

- In real fights, there is no room for fancy or complicated techniques; things must be kept simple.

- A real fight could happen at any time and without prior warning. There is no bowing or touching of gloves beforehand.

- Aggressive dialogue often precedes any real fight.

- Real fights are damn scary and extremely violent, no holds barred affairs. They are therefore not enjoyable in the slightest (unless violence is your thing).

So we can see that dojo sparring differs greatly from real fighting, and if we are to train for the real thing, we have to change our methods of training and sparring.

I am not of course saying that traditional dojo sparring doesn't have a place. People train for different reasons, so all types of sparring have their place in the dojo.

If you wish to train for real self-defense, however, then you must make the adjustments to your training methods so you are better able to deal with the real thing.

No matter how real you make your sparring, it will never be real enough, simply because you have to incorporate certain safety measures into it.

Making the training exactly like the real thing just defeats the object of training in the first place.

. . .

If we went all out, every sparring session would be a potentially life-threatening encounter. There still has to be control, and this is the fatal flaw in training for the real thing.

Inevitably you will have to wear protective gear, eliminate the use of specific techniques like groin strikes and eye gouges, and probably train on comfortable mats instead of concrete.

These flaws and limitations don't present too much of a problem as long as you are aware of them, and you factor them into your training.

If you happen to be wearing heavy boxing gloves, for instance, then be aware that in reality, you wouldn't be able to cover your face with them (because you wouldn't have them on), and your strikes would be much more effective without them on. You could also grapple without gloves. These are things you need to be aware of when sparring for the street.

So you have to make these changes in your training to make it more realistic, you get away from the usual form of dojo sparring and consider the conditions that exist in a real fight scenario.

Most importantly, you have to adjust your mindset and go from thinking about scoring points or submissions for competition to thinking about properly subduing and damaging a real attacker in the pavement arena.

The Pre-Emptive Strike

Most martial artists get it all wrong when it comes to self-defense. They think they can wait for someone to attack them and deftly handle that attack by using one of the many techniques they have been taught to do at their dojo, techniques that work so well in practice but in reality, will most likely not work anywhere near as well.

The reason these techniques don't work is that dojo fighting and real fighting are two different things. The arenas are different; the participants are different; and most important of all, *you* are different.

Live situations are vastly more pressurized and dangerous affairs, and they contain many more variables than one can hope to replicate in the dojo, which is why, in street self-defense, it pays to keep things as simple as possible.

I'll go one further and say that it pays even more to pre-empt an opponent's attack with one of your own. Hit them before they hit you, in other words.

And before we go any further here, I know what you're thinking: *"What about the law? Won't I get prosecuted for initiating an attack?"*

The short answer to that is no, not usually. The law these days is very open to the concept of pre-emptive attack, as long as you can show that an attack on your person was imminent.
    If you can show that you tried to calm the situation with dialogue and did all you could to dissuade an opponent from persisting with their aggression, then you should be okay in the eyes of the law.

It is extremely unwise to wait for someone to attack you before you put up a defense. When you allow an attack to happen, you not only lose control of the situation (because you have given your attacker the advantage), but you will also find it very difficult to defend once things kick-off.

I know this from experience in bouncing. You'll end up badly beaten up or rolling around the floor with the possibility of your opponents mates showing up to help kick your head in.

In a street self-defense situation, it is much easier to strike your opponent and then make your escape if possible. At the very least, taking the initiative will allow you to put in a few more strikes to finish an opponent while they are still dazed from the first strike. But as I say, it's always best to run from the situation if at all possible. Why hang around to attract more trouble?

Your pre-emptive strike should be one you are comfortable with and well-practiced in. My preference is the right hook or the right cross to the jaw, both of which will knock an opponent out if done correctly. At the very least, it will daze them enough for me to run.

To give yourself a further advantage, ask your opponent a question before you hit him. "How's *your mother doing?*" or something along those lines will do. The idea is to engage their brain and distract them from what is coming next, which is your strike to their jaw or slap to the face, whatever you wish to use.

Whatever technique you choose, make sure you are well-practiced in it. Spend a lot of time just honing that one technique and getting it right so you will have the power to knock an opponent down when the time comes.

You have no reason to wait to be attacked if that attack is inevitable. Take the initiative and get in a well-timed pre-emptive strike, then dart away in the confusion.

In a street self-defense situation, the pre-emptive strike is usually the wisest choice, especially when you are left with no other option. It is certainly better than waiting to be attacked.

• • •

Basic Strategies

What follows is a list of pointers outlining some things you should be aware of when you are defending against an attack. This information will help to keep you out of harm's way.

1. Try To Calm The Situation Down. If things are getting heated, always attempt to calm things down a bit before you resort to violence.

Look your antagonist in the eye and resist the temptation to let your anger get the better of you because this will only aggravate the situation and hasten the oncoming violence.

Stay calm and logically try to diffuse the situation. Smile even. Show your antagonist you have no interest in fighting. The calmer you come across, the more put off your antagonist will be, only because it will seem like you have nothing to prove, and you will, therefore, seem more dangerous to him.

It's the quiet ones you always have to be wary of, after all. Thugs look for fear in a person. They feed of it. Don't give them the satisfaction of knowing you are scared, even if that's the case. Stay stone cold.

2. Always Look For An Escape. The minute you think you will be attacked, start looking for an escape. If you can run, then run. Even if things have kicked off, keep looking for that escape.

I know a friend who was attacked by three guys from behind. He was pushed down in the street, and they all went at him at once. My friend was able to kick out with his legs from the ground to keep his attackers at bay, though. The first chance he got, he was on his feet and away running, saving himself from further hurt.

It's never too late to run.

3. Balance. Maintaining your balance is key to effective street self-defense. Without good balance, an opponent can easily knock you over or, at the very least, control your movement easier.

It is therefore important that you keep a good steady stance with the legs about shoulder-width apart and the feet turned slightly inwards, the very stance you've been practicing all these years in the dojo. Keeping a good fighting stance will allow you to strike properly and apply technique easier.

4. Distance. Next to balance, controlling the distance between you and your opponent is probably the single biggest thing you can do to survive a street altercation.

Don't allow your attacker to close the gap between you and him unless that is what you want to happen.

Use the fence technique if he is just being aggressive. If he is coming at you with a flurry of punches, use your kicks to keep him away from you, at a distance where he can't land any punches.

Likewise, if he is trying to kick you, close him down and apply a choke or takedown, put him on the ground where he can't hit you.
    The same applies with weapons. Most weapons require a certain distance to work properly. Blunt objects, like pool cues or bottles, need to be swung. Closing the distance will stop this from happening. Trap his arms so he can't swing the weapon, rendering it useless.

Care must be taken with knives, which can still injure from a closed position.

Guns can be dealt with in the same manner. The closer you are to the gun, the easier it will be to control it. Again, great care must be taken to make sure the gun is not pointed towards you as your attacker can still pull the trigger.

5. Assume Your Attacker Has A Weapon. If you always assume that your attacker has a weapon, you won't be too surprised if one appears.

The most common street weapon is the knife, and they come in all shapes and sizes, so sometimes you will see what appears to be a fist coming towards you, but actually, there is a small blade in that hand that you can hardly see. If you see your opponent reach into their jacket or pockets, close them down immediately before they have time to either pull the weapon or use it.

Concealed weapons are so common these days it would be foolish not to consider the possibility that an attacker is armed in some way. Train against weapons in the dojo, so you get a feel for them and don't be too scared by them.

6. Make It Difficult For An Attacker To Hit You. If your attacker punches with his right hand, try to move to their right side; and if they lead with the left, move to their left.

Positioning yourself to the outside of your opponent makes it harder for him to hit you, and easier for you to counter strike.

If you can get his back, then all the better because you can then kick the back of his knee and take him down.

The same applies if your attacker is trying to kick you. Move to the outside.

7. Use Your Surroundings. Put something between you and your attacker to stop him from getting at you. Cars are very good for this. They will still probably chase you around, but at least you'll have time to assess the situation better or buy yourself valuable time to think or make an escape.

Walls are beneficial when there are multiple opponents. Putting your back against a wall ensures no one will move around behind you and pull you to the ground or hit you from behind, leaving you one less thing to worry about.

8. Improvise Weapons. Again, this is using your surroundings to your advantage. Slamming an attacker against a wall or making him hit the concrete floor will take a lot of the fight out of them and do them a fair amount of damage at the same time.

Also, pick up whatever is lying around, especially with more than one attacker on the scene, things like bottles, pieces of wood, stones, anything that you can use as a makeshift weapon.

Sometimes the fact you even have something in your hand is enough to deter an attacker from going any further. Weapons put the odds back in your favor.

The only thing you have to careful of is your attacker disarming you and using the same weapon against you. Keep your wits about you at all times to ensure this doesn't happen.

9. Stay of The Ground. Never go to the ground unless you really have to. Going to the ground with an attacker will leave you in a vulnerable position, especially if he has mates with him. They'll just run over and start kicking you, and then you'll be beaten.

I've even seen fights were strangers who have nothing to do with the attack have run over and started kicking guys on the ground. So always try to finish an opponent standing up.

The only one who should go the ground is him when you've finished with him.

10. Target Your Opponent's Vulnerable Areas. Don't just blindly lash out at your attacker; target the areas on his body that will hurt him the most. Areas like the eyes, throat, groin, knee, shin, anywhere that will cause the most damage and stop the attack quickly.

With more than one attacker, it is even more important to stop them quickly so you can move on to deal with the next one. The quicker you put them down, the quicker it will all be over.

Street self-defense Techniques

As I've already mentioned, there are many techniques that you can use if attacked, depending on the type and ferocity of the attack.

I do not intend to exhaustively list them all here, not just because there are so many but also because many of them are inappropriate for live situations.

I therefore won't be laying out some nice step-by-step photos showing how to apply a complicated arm lock. That would be wasting my time and yours.

Instead, I will run through the basic techniques that you will be able to use to good effect without having to think too much about them or train for years to learn.

I'm talking here about simple punching, kicking, locking, and takedown techniques that require the minimum of movement and coordination to get right.

So let's look at those techniques and how to apply them in different situations.

Punching/Striking Techniques

These would include: Jabs, hooks, crosses, palm heel strikes, power slaps, elbow strikes, finger jabs, and hammer fists. These are all easy to learn and are most effective against any opponent.

Kicking Techniques

All kicks should be kept low to avoid losing balance. Kicking techniques would include: front snap kicks, side kicks, roundhouse kicks as well as heel stomps and knees.

Throws/Takedowns

These would include: hip throws, sweeps, some head throws, and any technique that involves taking your opponent off balance or using Tai Sabaki to redirect them. The simpler you keep things here, the better.

Chokes/Strangles

Chokes and strangles are excellent for self-defense and can be applied in a number of ways, from the front or back or on the ground. Caution must be exercised when using these techniques because it is very easy to crush someone's windpipe or severely damage their neck.

Those then are the main techniques you should be concentrating on. Nothing fancy involved there, just straightforward techniques that work in almost any situation.

Practice the strikes and kicks on a bag or on focus pads, and also practice against a partner who is simulating attacking you. Timing and distance is very important when using these techniques, so practice against a moving target as much as possible.

The Vital Attack Points

Besides knowing how to hit an opponent, it is also beneficial to know *where* to hit an opponent. You want to be able to take an attacker out quickly and easily, so there is no point in just lashing out and hoping you drop them, you have to target specific areas of your attacker's body to take them down effectively.

Many areas of the body will hurt like hell if you hit them in the right way, but the problem is that you may not be able to accurately target these areas when under the extreme pressure of combat.

• • •

Areas like the eyes, groin, and knees are simple enough areas to attack in the heat of the moment but forget about smaller pressure point areas; you just won't have the presence of mind to target these.

Attacking the jaw of your opponent is probably your best bet in a real fight. If you can land a good, hard strike to an opponent's jaw, you will stand a good chance of dropping them (the jaw is a direct link to the brain) or, at the very least, distract them enough so you can make your getaway.

Don't even wait around to apply any finishing strikes, just run. Remember, self-preservation is the name of the game, not fighting.

Weapons

Weapons are becoming more and more common in street fighting today, especially knives, so it pays to keep your awareness about you when you're involved in an altercation.

Always assume that your attacker has a weapon so you won't be caught unaware if one is produced.

If you do find yourself looking down the wrong end of a blade, my first advice to you would be to run if at all possible.

Failing that, look around you and pick up whatever isn't nailed down and hurl it at your attacker, then run.

If you have no option but to face off with your attacker, then all you can do is your best.

. . .

With knives, I hesitate to say that you should expect to get cut because going into a knife altercation with such a defeatist attitude will not help you any.

In saying that, you should still have it in the back of your mind that there is a very real chance you will receive a cut of some description. Expect to subdue the attack by all means, but don't be too shocked if you get cut.

Longer range weapons like sticks and chains and the like are easy enough to defend against because all you have to do is stay out of range and then quickly close the distance the first chance you get.

Longer range weapons are rendered useless when they can't be swung, so just get in close to your attacker and either disarm them or put them down straight away before they get the chance to create that distance again.

God forbid someone should pull a gun on you, but these can be defended against also like any other weapon, though the risk factor in doing so is a lot higher.

If someone pulls a gun, my advice is to do what they say. Trying to disarm someone with a gun is extremely risky. If all they want is your wallet, then give it to them. Only engage if it looks like you will get shot, and there is nothing else you can do about it.

Once again, you want to close the distance because doing so will take away much of the guns effectiveness. Guns are a lot less deadly at close range and can be easier controlled.

You should always try to run from weapons first, but if you no choice but to face off against them, then use what is lying around to improvise your own weapons—chairs, bottles, tables, anything that you can pick up and throw or use as a shield. Just be extra careful and make it your mission to put the guy down as quickly as possible and make sure he doesn't get back up again to have another go.

That's it for the strategies and tactics. All this information has to be assimilated and then integrated into your training and general lifestyle to be effective. Practice all the time to get good at using the various techniques and also get used to confrontation in itself.

In the next section, we will look at the aftermath of street confrontations, the consequences, and the effect they can have on your psyche and behavior.

SIX

Aftermath

If you have been assaulted or have successfully defended yourself against an assault, there will always be consequences of some description that you will have to deal with.

Violent encounters are rarely simple affairs that you can walk away from as if nothing has happened. Let's look at the possible consequences of violence that you may have to deal with.

Post-Assault Adrenaline

After a violent encounter, you will most likely find yourself suffering from adrenal-induced Tachypsychia.

Symptoms of this condition include time distortion, time loss, memory distortion, and memory loss. You may also find yourself shaking, and you will feel very wired as the adrenalin courses through you. In part, this is also due to your mind producing fear and dread over the consequences of what happened.

. . .

Street Survival Guide: Self Defense Awareness, Avoidance And Fighting...

Just accept that you can handle whatever consequences come at you and move on. Don't let slow-release adrenaline eat you up. Get rid of it by going running or hitting a bag, anything that will release it and stop it from building up in your system.

Having To Deal With The Law

It is highly likely, as we have already discussed, that you will have to deal with the law afterward, and if you do, you will have to give a statement about what happened.

You must be very careful here, though, because the Tachypsychia described above also leads to the innate urge to talk and blabber, if only to explain your actions.

The problem with this is that it makes it hard to give an objective statement to the police. Your statement will most likely be inaccurate because of this, which won't do you any favors when you have to stand up in court six months down the line and defend your actions.

If you don't feel you can make an accurate statement so soon after, then you are well within your rights to hold off till the next day. At the very least, you can insist on having a lawyer beside you while you are giving your statement.

Police being police will usually try to push for a quick conclusion to events, and they will try various tactics to make this happen, including leaving you alone for long periods, perhaps holding you in a cell and they may even tell you that you will go to prison for what you have done.

Under such pressure, it is very easy to tell them what they want to hear so you can get out of there and get home. So be very clear on your rights and insist that you see a lawyer before making any statements.

Revenge Attacks

Even if you subdue an attacker, there is always the chance that that person will exact their revenge at a later date. If they don't do the deed themselves, then they will pay someone else to do it for them.

I know of a few cases where this has happened, where people have been walking home one night, and they have been blind-sided by a waiting attacker. Often, there are weapons involved in these kinds of revenge attacks. Baseball bats are a common weapon of choice for such attacks because they do plenty of damage pretty quickly, and they are guaranteed to teach someone a lesson.

So be aware that you could spend quite a while looking over your shoulder after an attack, wondering when (if at all) the revenge is going to come.

Like I have already said, the best thing you can do is accept whatever consequences there are and also accept that you can deal with whatever comes your way. There is no point in living in fear and letting slow-release adrenaline poison your system.

Just remember that you can handle anything if you convince yourself of this fact, even revenge attacks.

Final Words

What I have tried to do here in this short guide is offer some sound advice on the subject of street self-defense, and while the information given here is by no means comprehensive, I hope it will at least help you get clear on how best to approach the very serious subject of personal protection.

I believe everyone should know how to defend themselves and their family in this day and age, which is why I wrote this guide in the first place, and I hope by reading it, you will get some benefit from it.

In the end, it is up to you to train yourself and to expand your knowledge base so you are as prepared as possible for any possible violent encounters you may find yourself in.

Only you can be responsible for your self-protection. I'll leave you with a sound piece of advice given by Geoff Thompson that cuts through the bullshit and all the hordes of other advice given on self-defense:

Learn to hit fucking hard...

Appendix: 20 Things You Should Know About Real Fighting

1. They happen fast and when you least expect it.

2. If attacked, you will most likely get hurt.

3. Fighting is not pretty.

4. The chances are high that you will have to defend against more than one attacker.

5. If you want to survive, hit back.

6. You will feel fear—learn how to deal with it.

7. You will have to focus on surviving.

8. You will have to react very quickly.

9. Your physical response must be fueled by self-preservation. Feelings don't come into it.

10. Most likely, no one will help you.

11. The police will not come and help you.

Appendix: 20 Things You Should Know About Real Fighting

12. The law will be against you.

13. To stand the best chance, you must be able to control the distance between you and your attacker.

14. Never go to the ground unless you have to because…

15. You never know who else will come along and attack you.

16. Always assume your attacker has a weapon, especially a knife, so you won't get caught unaware.

17. Be aggressive—sheep don't beat wolves.

18. Do what you have to do to survive the attack—better to be judged by twelve than carried by six.

19. Don't be afraid to use your surroundings to your advantage—use the walls, the concrete floor, anything you can use as a weapon, and that will quickly damage an attacker.

20. Your attacker will dictate when the attack is over, not you.

Why let someone else dictate your chances of survival? It is up to you to be prepared for such a situation and to control it when it happens.

Your life may depend on it.

Further Resources

What follows is a list of books and websites that you can use to further your knowledge on the subject of self-defense. They are all excellent resources and they are listed here in no particular order.

Books

Living the Martial Way : A Manual for the Way a Modern Warrior Should Think—Forest E. Morgan

Fear—Geoff Thompson

Dead Or Alive—Geoff Thompson

Sharpening the Warriors Edge: The Psychology & Science of Training—Bruce Siddle

The Flinch—Julien Smith

Warrior Mindset— Dr. Michael Asken, Loren W. Christensen, Dave Grossman

Meditations on Violence: A Comparison of Martial Arts Training & Real World Violence—Rory Miller

Further Resources

Facing Violence—Rory Miller

Self-Defense Fundamentals: A Guide to Making Yourself a Hard Target—Neal Martin

One Small Request

Can I ask you do me a small favour? If you have read this whole book, could you please leave a review on your favorite book vendor? Reviews sell books, and I'd like to hear your feedback anyway, even if you hated the book. Honest reviews are what matters. Thanks in advance.

About the Author

Rory Christensen has been a practicing martial artist for over thirty years now. He is a 5th degree black belt in Goju Ryu and a 2nd degree black belt in Shotokan karate. He has also trained in various other arts, including Kenpo, Jujitsu, Aikido and Kali. He resides in California with his wife and three daughters.

His other books include: *Mind Training for Martial Artists*, and *Drills For self-defense: A Martial Artists Guide to Reality self-defense.*

Made in the USA
Middletown, DE
11 July 2023

34893864R00040